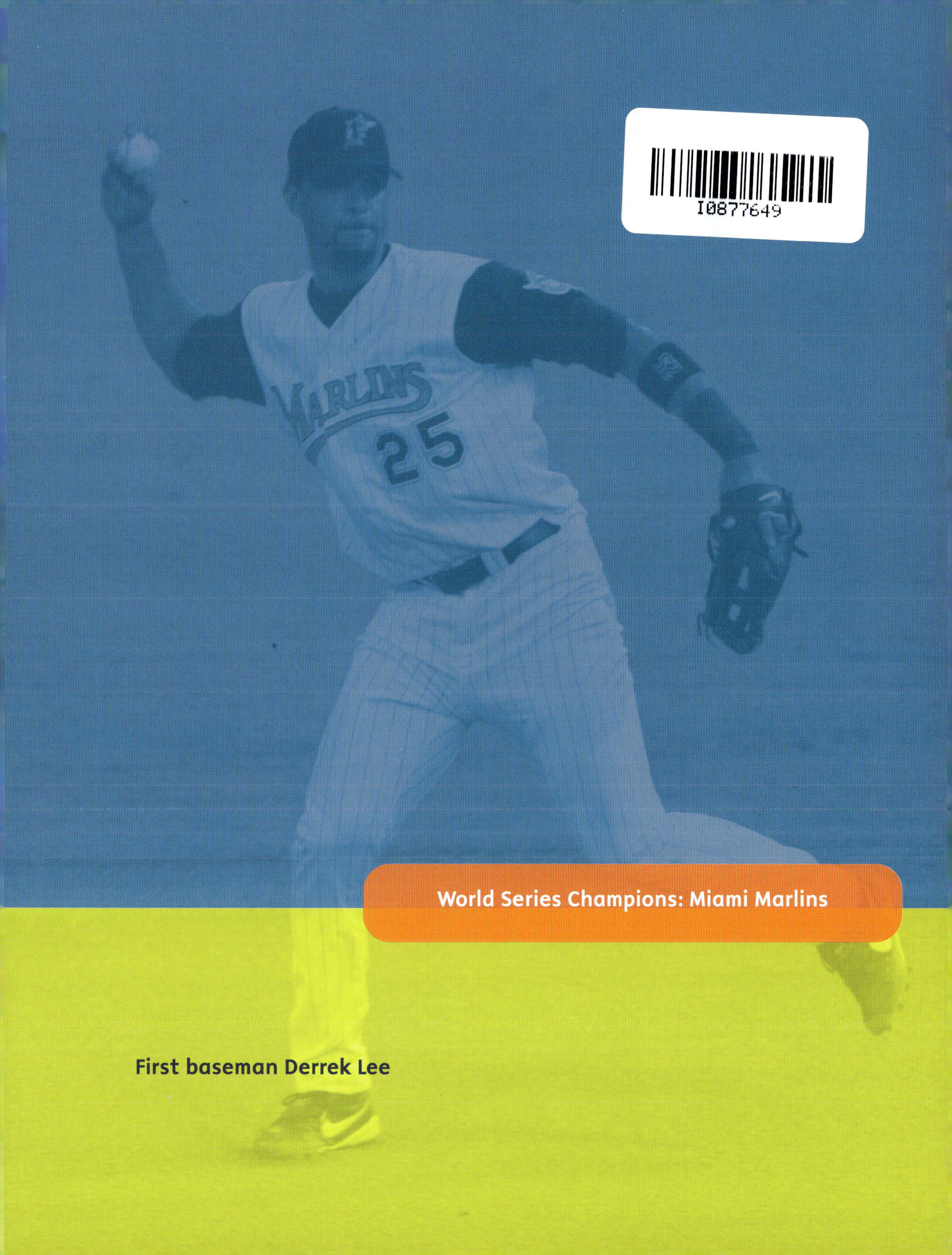

World Series Champions: Miami Marlins

First baseman Derrek Lee

Pitcher Sandy Alcantara

WORLD SERIES CHAMPIONS

MIAMI MARLINS

MEGAN COOLEY PETERSON

CREATIVE SPORTS

CREATIVE EDUCATION / CREATIVE PAPERBACKS

Published by Creative Education and Creative Paperbacks
P.O. Box 227, Mankato, Minnesota 56002
Creative Education and Creative Paperbacks are imprints of The Creative Company
www.thecreativecompany.us

Art Direction by Tom Morgan
Book production by Ciara Beitlich
Edited by Joe Tischler

Photographs by Alamy (Tribune Content Agency LLC), AP Images (Wilfredo Lee, Lynne Sladky), Corbis (Stephen Green, Eliot Schechter, Matthew Stockman), Dreamstime (Giovanni Gagliardi), Getty (Al Bello, Justin Casterline, Mitchell Layton, Ronald C Modra, Jasen Vinlove/Miami Marlins, Doug Pensinger)

Library of Congress Cataloging-in-Publication Data
Names: Peterson, Megan Cooley, author.
Title: Miami Marlins / Megan Cooley Peterson.
Description: Mankato, MN : Creative Education and Creative Paperbacks, [2024] | Series: Creative sports. World Series champions | Includes index. | Audience: Ages 7-10 | Audience: Grades 2-3 | Summary: "Elementary-level text and engaging sports photos highlight the Miami Marlins' MLB World Series wins, plus sensational players associated with the professional baseball team such as Sandy Alcantara."-- Provided by publisher.
Identifiers: LCCN 2023008244 (print) | LCCN 2023008245 (ebook) | ISBN 9781640268272 (library binding) | ISBN 9781682773772 (paperback) | ISBN 9781640009974 (pdf)
Subjects: LCSH: Miami Marlins (Baseball team)--History--Juvenile literature. | World Series (Baseball)--History--Juvenile literature.
Classification: LCC GV875.M47 P47 2024 (print) | LCC GV875.M47 (ebook) | DDC 796.357/6409759381--dc23/eng/20230227
LC record available at https://lccn.loc.gov/2023008244
LC ebook record available at https://lccn.loc.gov/2023008245

Printed in China

2003 World Series Champions

Pitcher Josh Beckett

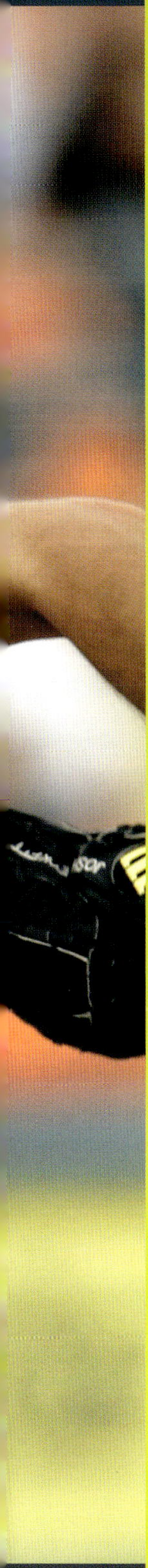

CONTENTS

Home of the Marlins

The city of Miami, Florida, sits along the Atlantic Ocean. Many people visit the city's beaches and clubs. They also cheer on the Marlins baseball team. Players thrill fans at LoanDepot Park, their home **stadium**.

The Miami Marlins are a Major League Baseball (MLB) team. They play in the National League (NL) East Division. Their **rivals** are the Atlanta Braves. All MLB teams try to win the World Series to become champions.

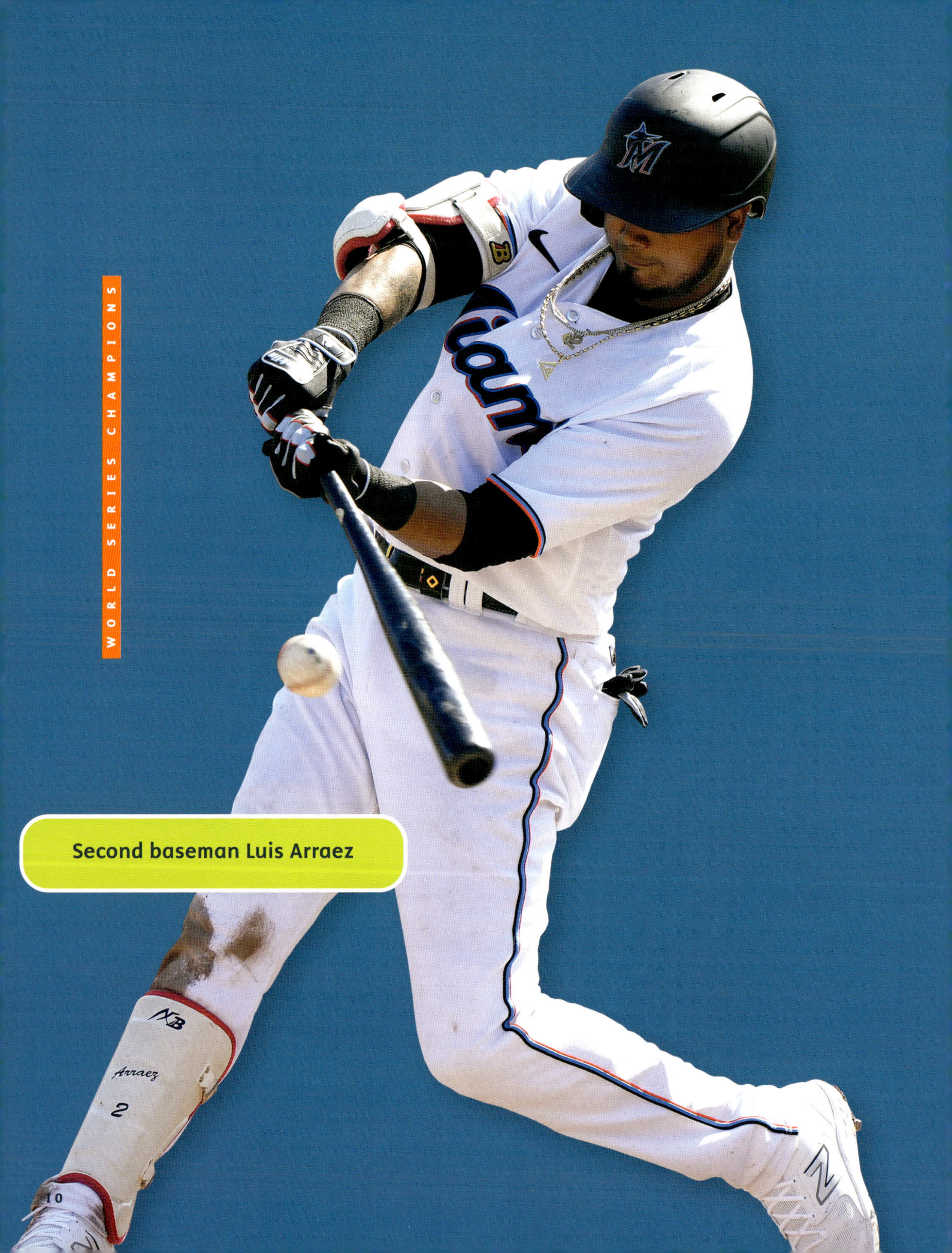

Second baseman Luis Arraez

Naming the Marlins

The Marlins' owner named the team after one of his favorite fish to catch. Marlins have pointed, spear-like noses. They swim in the ocean near Miami. The team used to be called the Florida Marlins. Today, many fans simply call them "The Fish."

Outfielder Gary Sheffield

Marlins History

The Marlins joined the National League in 1993. Jeff Conine got hit after hit. Charlie Hough struck out batters. But the Marlins lost more games than they won for the first few years.

The Marlins got a new manager in 1997. Jim Leyland led his team to the **playoffs** that year. Pitcher Liván Hernández and outfielder Gary Sheffield helped them win playoff games. The team beat the San Francisco Giants and the Atlanta Braves.

The Marlins faced the Cleveland Indians in the World Series. Edgar Rentería hit a **walk-off** single in the 11th inning of Game 7. The Marlins were champions!

Shortstop Edgar Rentería

Pitcher Charlie Hough

The Marlins dropped to last place the next year. The next few seasons didn't go well either. The team got its spark back during the 2003 season. They made it to their second World Series. Few people thought the Marlins could best the Yankees. But they did. They beat New York in six games.

Other Marlins Stars

The Marlins have had many star players. Pitcher Josh Beckett was named Most Valuable Player (MVP) of the 2003 World Series. Third baseman Mike Lowell played in three All-Star Games. First baseman Derrek Lee smashed 129 homers.

Second baseman Luis Castillo's **hustle** on the field made him a star. He won three Gold Gloves as a Marlin. The best fielders win this award.

Second baseman Luis Castillo

Outfielder Giancarlo Stanton

Outfielder Giancarlo Stanton joined the team in 2010. In 2012, he blasted a homer that sailed almost 500 feet. He won the NL MVP Award in 2017.

In 2022, pitcher Sandy Alcantara won the Cy Young Award. The best pitchers win it. All-Star infielders Jean Segura and Luis Arraez joined the team in 2023. Fans are ready for another Marlins' World Series championship!

About the Marlins

Started playing: 1993

League/division: National League, East Division

Team colors: black, blue, red, grey

Home stadium: LoanDepot Park

WORLD SERIES CHAMPIONSHIPS:

1997, 4 games to 3 over Cleveland Indians

2003, 4 games to 2 over New York Yankees

Miami Marlins website: www.mlb.com/marlins

Glossary

hustle—the ability to move fast or try hard to get a job done

playoffs—games that the best teams play after a regular season to see who the champion will be

rival—a team that plays extra hard against another team

stadium—a building with tiers of seats for spectators

walk-off—a base hit that brings in the winning run

Shortstop Jean Segura

Index